MORTAL THOUGHTS

Also by Michael R. Lane

MORTAL THOUGHTS

~Poems~

Michael R. Lane

BARE BONES PRESS
P.O. Box 9653, Seattle, WA 98109

Published by Bare Bones Press, Seattle, Washington.

Design: Bare Bones Press
Production: Bare Bones Press
Cover Art: Monika Younger

Bare Bones Press
P.O. Box 9653
Seattle, WA 98109

www.michaelrlane.net
www.michaelrlane.com

Third Edition: September 2023

Dedication

To the educators and distillers of creative writing, art and music who have enriched my life beyond compensation thank you for helping me to see that the stars are within reach even if you have to stand on the tips of your toes to touch them.

POET'S NOTE

The idea for *Mortal Thoughts* — not in name but in body — began taking shape for me in November 2015. I — like so many others — wade in the erratic waters of intellect and mortality and all of the precious cognitive and ethereal lakes, rivers and streams that congregate between. I have been blessed to hone those temporal thoughts into poetry over the years, an extraordinary written art form that for whatever reason arises in me during my most mystifying times. Why does poetry so readily lend itself to the essence of transcendental deliberations, stoic cogitations and silly musings? The riposte is as simple as dreaming and as complex as mud. It does. For me, the answer begins and ends there, unveiling the journey as in the title, "Mortal Thoughts."

> Staring skyward at night-light
> flickering stars yawn and wink
> royal blue canvas eclipses daylight
> moonlight on my bedspread plays. (1-4)

While the poems in this volume were written over a number of years — from the 1970s until the month of publication — the collection was originally compiled, edited and refined between February 2016 and June 2017. I hope you enjoy *Mortal Thoughts* as much as I did in its creation.

The language for the Second Edition of *Mortal Thoughts* is identical to the First Edition. Poetic forms for some poems have been modified from their original publication to better suit the poet's intended cadence.

Contents

MORTAL THOUGHTS

A Writer's Hope Chest

That mailbox was my hope chest.
Monday through Saturday,
I insert my key with the fragile possibility
that this will be the time someone,
    somewhere
will unequivocally, state in a letter,
"We want to publish your work."
This time there will be more than bills
or unwarranted solicitations,
    or air,
or an SASE weighted with my forsaken material,
accompanied by a brooding standard rejection slip.
Maybe …
    just maybe …
this one will click,
uplifting the promise that I am a writer worth reading,
and all of the reclusive years of creation and faith
will not have been in solitary vain.

Rhyming Poetry

What is a poem
that does not rhyme?
Does it lack the essence
of pure poetic grace?

Has it no backbone
Or the substantial will
to exhibit the message
of a people's plight?

Will there be futures
for such a beast?
Or must it tremble and die
at one's calloused feet?

Is there credibility
in poem absent rhyme?
"The Vision of Judgment"
is not solely mine.

Not all is lost
when one stops to think
iambic pentameters
are not meant to be.

For balance and tone
should in free verse exist
like poetic bliss
in a sunrise or a kiss.

Sedate as moonlight
eyeing nature's breasts,
poetry is not words which rhyme
but what those words project.

Channel Surfing

The game was over;
our team had been vanquished,
the random channel surfing begun
in concert with our persistent
bemoaning armchair breakdowns
of our insightful pros and cons
of the modern gladiator contest
we had passionately witnessed.

No one was really watching the tube
once the warriors had left the arena;
no one was actually talking to each other,
our foamy dialogues having washed away
without the common blood ground
of martial parties sparking
our spirited competitive fires.

Our existence was independent
yet dependent;
void, yet immersed
in an alcohol drenched, snack filled
world of excess trash talking
aboard a testosterone train
that had ground to a halt.

The game was over.
Our brittle union was swiftly dissolving
like granulated camaraderie
in a boiling lethargy brew until …
another campaign loomed on the big bright screen
a generous offering from the omniscient cable gods
of blessed colorful sight and sound and conflict.

The invading ether of boredom evaporated
the malleable epoxy of rejuvenation. Hardened,
we leaned forward in party unison
mesmerized by the beckoning siren call
of delicious combat on the near horizon —
the voices and scenes drew us into the clash
like unfulfilled men into the arms of lust.

We hoisted our sails and headed for open waters
upon a male bonding warship of modern sport.

Winter

Bleak and cramped

skeleton trees
destitute plants

frost bite winds
eternal nights

crystal latticed
flakes in flight

melancholy,

kitten curled
by the fire.

Downtown Christmas Lights

Through clear foggy glass,
soft lights decorate barren trees
sparkling twice and thrice
through dismal winter night
illuminating, a dramatic sweep
of kindred impoverished trees
appareled in relative décor.

As bundled humans
ignore their quaint existence
upward, they stretch
toward a royal blue carpet
of twinkling starlight sky
as if pointing to the icy heavens
in awe of the shimmering view.

Shaman

A weathered Native American
sitting on a wooden bench

near a metro bus stop
in his blue baseball cap

shiny silver jacket
spotted blue pants
mangled leather tennis shoes

with legs too short
to reach the sidewalk

reminded me of a shaman
standing atop a towering mountain,

his lofty arms
aimed toward the heavens

proud, fearless, mighty;

knowing the pathway to God.

Human Jingle

That wonderfully nourishing sound
of the hollow becoming full,
swirling cylindrically around
as an H_2O whirlpool
in a saint's rheumy pupils
obscured by cataracts;

as we sleep the cattle's sleep
and dream of mice and men,
glaring at our journey back
to undo the undone deeds,
leapfrog toward human truths,
the glass slippers of our youth;

forever we wander wonder
somewhere out beyond ourselves;
let us not put hope asunder
while exploring universal worlds,
traversing paths of intimate valleys
ascending aureate mountain peaks;

borne in an ocean of descant knowledge
a painted hawk in stalwart flight
observes our squirming rigid mass
treading to avoid its cloudy depths,
yet are we not all a melodious sum
of our resonant parts — plus one?

Cars

Cars skimming highways
born of concrete and asphalt
guided by striped markings
and channeled by steel;

people survive in these mechanized cocoons,
pipelines to redundant or desired destinations;
a binding motor contract with an outside world

defined by humans
ordered by humans
maintained by humans

common hominids profess beliefs and worship
gods who shelter from harm and misery
deities who respond to whims and necessities,
divinities contracting destined paths;

how do I wedge into this puzzle of mortality?
This limbo is spawned of consciousness and dreams.
How are my irregular pieces shaped?
Is there afterlife after ceded bachelorhood,
marriage, children, mid-life, ancient?

What is a car but an apparatus that streaks
through the mystic maze of living years
gobbling hordes of earthly real estate,
fuming gaseous exhausts of neutral memoirs?

If I stumbled upon clarity, what would it denote?
To whom and why and what would it alter?
If I managed to pinpoint specifics from haze,
drain precision from ether existence,
what would it signify in the end?

No drug replaces healthy natal disposition
yet we seek the elixir outside of ourselves;
a spark to inflame humanity, intellect, and egos;
a panacea for better, stronger, faster, smarter.

It is the winding road on our undulating journey
illuminated with lamp posts of our own choosing,
embroidered with signs of our own making,
tracked with faith before the screeching halt.

This Is Not a Rap

This is not a Rap —
it is a poem
a simple leaf of eloquent liquid word expression
endeavoring to articulate, communicate and elaborate
upon that which is and is not
utilizing language on paper and nothing more —
no plugs, no outlets, no power supplies;
electrical currents powered only by the mind
minus a droning backbeat or narcissistic performer,
absent blatant marketing or manufactured muse.
Not essential are rapid-fire deliveries or brusque attitudes
to drag its meaning into the light —
my voice and appearance are not significant to its purpose
vanity is not at the core of its claim
mixers and microphones are not compulsory
no crew or cast or concert is prevalent
you do not have to put your hands up
you do not have to extol your appreciation
with shouts, yells, whistles, cellphones or applause;
you can read it for yourself by yourself
derive your own cadence and melody
or absorb its verses in silence if you choose;
broker from poetry what it humbly offers
and leave what remains for others
to decide for themselves
in their solemn hearts
in their intimate souls
what truth it may hold.

Babble Culture

A great deal said in our clamorous time
holds little spiritual import or humane worth —
babble entertainment and babble news
babble politics and babble religion,
their triviality masquerading as essential fodder
force-fed to us by attention starved whores
and gobbled up by our voracious cerebrums,
egotistical prostitutes bred by gold-greedy goblins
jockeying to squeeze through lead bars of gilded gates
for a chance to compete at bottom-line incest.

All of this vacuous gabble-sense
has net so little forward-sense
unless you count copious nonsense
that hazes our faculties and blots our divine;
our fragile foundations are mixed and cured,
fractured knowledge marbled with lime;
an edifice flawed with a technology facade
for many seem content to sup from the bottom
rather than embrace the kinetic art of wisdom
to fuel their flight to feast from the heavens.

Brotha, *Please*

The corner drug dealer called me brotha.
     He said he had what I needed.
I waved him off without eye contact.
     One of his clients shuffled toward me,
His body draped in tattered clothes,
     his hair a matted filth,
his unwashed skin plagued with
     cuts, bruises, scabs and sores
varied in degrees of destruction.
     "Can you spare some change, brotha?"
the client begged more than asked.
     His breath reeked of vomit.
His body smelled like a used toilet.
     With firm conviction I said, "No!"
continuing to walk, not making eye contact.
     I could feel his rheumy eyes follow me.
At a distance, I stopped and looked back.
     The client shuffled up to the drug dealer,
emptied his pockets into the hands
     of the one who called me brotha.
The drug dealer handed the shell of a man
     what he needed, then shoved him away.
I continued to watch the zombie procession
     shuffle up to the dealer,
empty their pockets, praise him,
     then scurry away.
I had heard dealers refer to
     their clients as suckers and fools.
This person who called me brotha.
     This person who had what I needed.
This lie of brotherhood
     this mass murderer of
life and dreams who will be revered
     in films, videos, books and television
by those unknowing or indifferent about
     what their existence really means.

This purveyor of chemical genocide
     armed with a capitalist's dream
barren of ethics
     annihilates humanity
to feed his bottom line.
     He called me brotha.
He said he had what I needed.
     He is not my brotha.
He has nothing I need.

Body Count

Watch the world
people streaming everywhere
zombie troopers all around,
body count,
millions,
head count,
minimal.

Fact

Keep one thing in mind:
people may cheer the underdog
but they succumb to overdogs.

Spring

Buds and blossoms
season of songs
graceful sunlight
life reborn
fragrant air
mellow
fresh
rain dance time
feeds the flesh
of Mother Nature's
favorite nest.

Precipitation

Precipitation has no master.
It plummets or drifts from the heavens
uninhibited upon the world below.
Sometimes torrential as a waterfall,
other times as meek as mist.
It pools without permission upon
ice, oceans, lakes, rivers, streams,
farms, fields, meadows, towns, cities,
landfills, minefields, plains, countries, borders,
human, animal, vegetable, mineral, alien,
without regard to consequences or jurisdictions;
without consideration of manmade rules or laws.

Have a Nice Day

"Have a nice day, and try to stay dry," the bus driver said.
I thanked her and stepped out onto the curb.
A steady drizzle threatened to upgrade to a downpour.
Dark clouds supported that speculation.
A few cold drops of rain spattered my face and hair.
I unbound my umbrella,
placing my thumb on the pushbutton to spring it open.
More cold droplets found their way to my flesh.
It felt refreshing,
a natural baptism,
stimulating, yet soothing.
I rebound my umbrella,
using it as a walking cane
for the remainder of my stroll home,
having a nice day, as the bus driver wished,
without staying dry.

Dreams

A spy who creeps into your mind
who you recognize with a sigh,
he opens his little bag of tricks
and out of them come things of wit.
The prayers, hopes, and smiles in time,
like the glorious sun at dawn, will shine
through the darkness of your closed eyes
and let the dreams that you find
pattern the sweet music of your mind.

Friend

"Stretch out your hand to me,"
a man once said,
"and I will be your friend, forever."

Veldt

A sinewy, tall, dark man raced across the bus station,
red knit cap, black tennis shoes, beige jacket, black jeans.
You could imagine him gliding
across an African veldt
covered in breechcloths;
African sun radiating on his blackberry skin,
a contemplative expression on his Warrior's face,
a calm focus in his clear chestnut eyes
as if visualizing the journey's end,
returning from battle or engaged in a hunt,
boldly striding home to family and friends.

Paradise Lost

Its heritage and birthplace are
descendant fables of Sanskrit parables

ablaze shards of galactic history
razor slice, stomp and erupt

belching molten lava vowels and
screeching consonants form firmament definitions

avalanche from blood drenched tongues
plunged into cosmic soup

defining our fragile eggshell planet
seeding our brittle providence

human paradox parasites infect
infinite commonsense nurtured balance

open ears absorb water drum rhythms,
staccato timetables of global history

open minds uncoil with quiet patient
shoals of ranting mystic messages
scrolled in ancient cerebral code

skittering brittle microcosmic embryo
third child born of a volcanic sun

asked to bear the fruit of creation
willing no longer to breast-feed its spawn.

The Promised Land

"Onward!"
echoes a voice,
resounding,
yet caring and clear.
"You should not fear.
Your time has come.
Rise and join us.
Know Wisdom and Truth,
Mercy and Freedom,
Joy and Peace.
They are all family here.
A place for all,
this is the Promised Land."
Still mortals cannot
sever life's cord with such ease.
Despite the mighty sword
hacking steadily,
offering no reprieve;
especially for those caring,
for another's despair.
They, not knowing beyond,
await Ecstasy's gates,
protecting virtuous spirits
from earthly primates.

Hobo

An emaciated man shoved a rusty shopping cart,
laboring as if ascending a mountain,
His goodwill reservoir crammed with survival goods
discovered from judicious urban foraging.
His long green coat stained and frayed.
Shredded black leather shoes striped his feet.
Brown paper bags gloved his hands,
old wrinkled bags resembled his face.

Bustling humans blessed with better fates
asked if any had change they could spare.
All responded with zero aide.
Discouraged, but unhindered, he stayed the course
toward a shelter of rest and rations
viewed only from behind his sad bleary eyes;
halting to rummage through trash can deposits,
mumbling, pushing, feet groping toward progress.

Drizzle was cool and gentle on my skin,
I felt guilty and ashamed for not having helped.
I should have spared him currency as he passed,
bathed in human waste, sour grapes, and urban decay.
A dollar is little to gift sustained existence,
his appearance older than prior homeless
I had witnessed — ancient, in fact,
gray sprouting from every visible place.

Maybe his origin was hobo fit and strong,
a nobler title than 'homeless' by any stretch,
riding the rails when he was young
and dreams of a better life were still to come.

Provisional Death

Have you ever wished to die?
not in a manner of suicide
but for a week or two,
a vacation
from the so-called
"real world,"
to check out of a rat race existence
and into a deep,
mysterious,
cannot be disturbed,
ten-foot deep slumber.

No More Sorrow

Come children of peace
to the bosom of love.
Lay your weary heads against
her ripened breast to sleep.

To sleep forever;
for that is what we trust
can still bring accord
when all else fails.

No more tears, no more sorrow,
are words not made from fiber and flesh,
a dim candle light cry of faith
from a faltering land, we momentarily possess.

Is it true someday all will cease
and we shall wistfully gaze
at that place from which dreams
have such mysterious beginnings?

Let us pray in earnest —
mercy is the manufacturer,
and our beliefs are not labeled
Made by Man.

Betrayal

Destiny: pliant, toothsome Destiny,
so many you have betrayed,
cunning promises lovelier than the rose
aqueous corpses pool in granite graves.

Empty roadways roll toward darkened tombs —
musty, dank caverns line the way;
blazon hot by inky flames
gushers spew dead dreams' remains.

Wails of light bombard your palace,
tears crash harsh inside your brain.
Heed you not to sadden spirits;
ignorance is bliss, your favorite saying?

How can life be this sightless?
Not to spy your grotesque plan?
Pith bewildered, longing, wingless,
laps food from wrinkled agony's tin.

Hope *is* comfort, time falsely consoles,
knowing every scheme and plan
treacherous, deceptive, butchering Destiny
boundless wonders are your intimate kin.

Tranquility

There is a precise calmness,
a sea breeze into a person's soul,
which channels in the dead of night
a disconcerting tranquility,
a welcomed respite,
for still-minded individuals
whose daily worries
have ceased for a time.

None can unequivocally state
from where it germinates,
snaking drowsily through the gray,
slithering cordially around the heart,
creating a temporary homestead
in some fecund berth
masquerading within ourselves
as empty space.

Who amongst us lives in such grace?

To Dust Shall We Return

Headstones protruding from soil and dirt
witnessed by angels in ancient heavens,

blind eye soothsayer foretells all futures
vanilla aroma illusion of the mind.

Drumming raindrops pound out a message
beyond the scope and reach of man;

the cold teeth of winter
the hot breath of summer
tip the scale of life upon each act.

Salt sea breezes prick dormant skin to life
awakening silent ticks of timed heartbeats,

asking the question, while knowing the answer:
has mankind really ennobled his being
from the animals of their ancestral creed?

Should one day our metamorphic planet be reduced
to firmament and gases and liquids once clear,

how will nature mark our extinction —
headstones afloat in marshy graves?

Information Exchange

For all we have created,
for all we've yet produced,
sound,
sight,
touch,
smell,
taste
are how we converse with others
and how we are communicated to.

Traffic

Roaring echoes of vehicular traffic
seep into serene homes
cultivating the sweep of civilization
migrating beings to and from.

Mechanical beasts populate urban forests,
swarm paved passages scoured into
unexploited fertile scenic landscapes
to lessen the trek of hominoids.

Artificial roadways delineated
with yellow and white lines
suffocate soil that nurtured
a much more native life.

The roads most traveled
exhibit the fewest signs
of nature in her virgin glory
of man in his greatest sublime.

Scratching

Gibberish with a backbeat
closeted himself away, groping:
revelations, absurdities, remorse, integrity,
impulses, decay, faculties, extraordinary,
getting paid and getting laid,
depth, honesty, realm, catharsis,
wit and wisdom, cultivation,
sage, fame and fortune,
celebrity, good, bad, indifferent,
dignity, vague, spectral, dazzle,
dull, profundity, ostentation, fervent,
silt, inspiration, pomp exhibitionism,
temperamental clarity dropped
in time to the cramped rhythm,
in time to the compacted beat.

I've Known Rivers

History formed rivers
of experience
in excavated lines
on his Ethiopian face:

Deep obvious places
content on form and shape.

Beginnings mated futures
over the waterfall of age,

and as Langston once said,
says as well he,
"I've known rivers …
and they've known me."

Grandma

Her body lay heavy
like a copper stone
in a flower print dress
atop the firm, queen size mattress.
Her face carved in shock,
astonishment chiseled in her cold gray eyes.
Light abundant filled the room
but did not dance;
instead, it blossomed down
from overhead lamps and
softly kissed her wrinkled flesh.
Tired and aged,
intending only a moment's peace,
never once suspicious,
from beneath the bed …
death would creep.

Death of a Star

Sunrise
Sunset
far beyond our reach,
simply light rays
in sighted eyes.

Arise at dawn,
night we sleep
hopes of future
young hearts keep.

Weaving straws
twilight minds
illuminating stars
radiate
shine
brightest
before they die.

Imagination

There is a brief spell of time
within the deepest darkness of night
when all lies calm and silent.
Stars and moon pour twilight beams
into a spot
where faith-filled souls converge
creating a pencil-thick rainbow.
Near this place heaven resides;
hell far beyond —
though unguarded
it has never been conquered
while many have sought
to unbridle its gifts.
If you are fortunate
to experience such a graceful moment,
relax,
close gently your eyes,
and listen
for a solitary tone,
the key to this magnificent,
wondrous place;
      Imagination.

Precious Gifts

Mortals,
understand
life is too short,
time, too valuable
love, too sweet
friends, too few
peace, too scarce
harmony, too frivolous
dreams, too real
to waste any and all.
They are but a few
of the precious gifts
bestowed upon us all.
      Do not squander them,
   humanity
enjoy.

Phase I

We're wrong to deal in absolutes
since life is not forthright
and man much more complex;
still, just to make life easier,
we try with ease to correct
— or change —
the frothy constitutions of
all, but with regret;
for life is ever changing
not always for the best.

Depression

Outside:
      trees loom brash and bold
      Afroed rolling mountain ranges
      ravens, robins, hawks and such
      perilously ride invisible winds.

      Billowy white patches float
      beneath the powder blue of sky,
      casting various tones of gold
      upon varied shades of green.

      Far in distance atop
      the spotty horizon's crest
      beams Serenity's doleful face;
      smiling contently, inviting all
      to her peaceful natural space.

      Calm with gentle appears the world
      outside the clear glass walls.

      Inside a silent mourner
      having interest not in class
      drapes his mind in total boredom;
      depression his mood does firmly grasp.

Destiny

Crawl, walk, run, hobble all
to the pounding on a time-full drum
grown weary from its rancid beat.

Hup, two, three, four,
cadence from the faceless voice
directing all, neglecting none,
toward their charted, destined course.

Soldiers in a life brigade
parrying thrusting steely blades
propagated by soldier Time,
forever and always the end sublime.

Yet its path not smooth nor clear
for in its wake the cold sharp steel
does pierce the soulful heart that fades,
dripping with life it beats alas
until none can trace its vibrant past.

Goodbye

Farewell kiss
tearful wave
we all have said goodbye

grade school friends
prom dance night
embraces last forever

summer days
winter nights
autumn leaves change colors

parents die
children cry
dreams bid fond adieu

within a blink
life's fires sink
descending into fate

before too long
I'll too be gone
accursed time won't wait.

Twilight

Peering skyward before dawn
flickering stars yawn and wink
royal blue canvas eclipsing daylight
raise an eyelid for all to see.

Good Morning

Good morning God,
nice to see you again.
You're looking almighty as always,
our golden sun a radiant spec
glistening in the dreamy pupil
of your universal eye;

did I mention how much I love you?
The last time I ventured into your garden
to pluck your fruit as we conversed.

If I neglected to expose my heart,
my sentience has made you conscious.
Since my being has no place
to mask from your supreme awareness;
and thanks for creating knowledge
that's so delicious to digest.

Inherent Ambiguities

What an ambiguous craft
poetry.

It requires relating
to persons anonymous

dreams
accounts
experiences

composed of
sounds
sights

sapor
scents
sensations

in words
inherent with
ambiguities of their own.

How then
does one pinpoint
what is actual?

Or more precisely
what is not.

Flattery

Always take flattery with a teaspoon of bitters.
It can come from the mouths of your enemies,
whether you deserve them or not.

Fatigue

There are two things I am plain tired of:
I'm tired of being poor,
and I'm tired of being tired.

Death

Reaching backward
wanting never to release,
a cringe of terror
the sudden shriek,
lost spirits burdened,
futures clear.

Death is here.

Unwelcome Visitor

Uneven breezes roll through open windows,
curtains float and flutter in their wake.
Moans of anguish carry them onward,
woman weep while men distress.

Glare they all at open casket,
lying rigid, still as glass.
Words are lost, shock greets horror,
life once was, now has passed.

"How'd it happen? Can't understand it?"
no one knew — "Why?" they asked.
Replies were spoken, all in sorrow,
"Unwelcome visitor," a breeze whispered back.

We All Must Fall

There are no stark realities
strolling our world of disbelief,
scraping the bonded body of sensibility
collapsed upon a thorny bed,
dispersed through fields of sociability
humans tap the keg of dread.
Scope of minds trapped in visions
soaped to the throat with scrupulous hope.
Slapped on the hand
pinched on the cheek
spanked by a weed
gouged in the eyes
punched in the teeth —
such is the brutality and want of rage
searching through heaps of wasted flesh,
dumped by Atlantis upon fertile lands,
scooped from phantom barrels
then flung to earth
by ghostly hands.
Anonymous victims supply only questions;
answers surface through the muck.
Lurking spies behind tree trunks
whispered conversations
giggle and spit and draw blood.
Hazardous memories rip out the soul,
exploit constellations as solid as light,
and glisten as processed gold.
Sting, stung, stinging
trip, fall, fell
and lift up singing
in harmony
with the bells of hell.

Phase II

We're wrong to be so narrow
with our petty, worthless ways,
scratching out our meager livings,
judging all by surface spies.

True, it is much easier
than the scrutinizing eye,
grasping person, grouped with problems,
trying all, both fair and wise.

We find this task too daunting,
let waste our precious time,
fragile life, proven innocent
until proven otherwise.

Have we become so shallow
as to have no need for thought?
When a life based on trust
is denied benefit of doubt?

Dig a grave both deep and wide
to bury that which we have lost;
a sole factor of humankind,
known as the bicameral mind.

A useless grayish glob,
reduced to prehistoric fodder
once used for lucid thought
wring dry the muddied blotter.

Life is not some forthright vision
and man much more complex,
still just to make life easier
we seek simple epitaphs;

Steering frothy constitutions
toward a life that we see fit,
since humans are perpetually evolving
not always for the best.

Creative Writing

There is nothing new to write
regarding the human experience;
no masterful epics to scribe
no world-beating poems to gestate
no women to seduce
no men to intrigue
no children to inspire —
it is all diminished
gone
warped
commercialized
vanquished
cruising the dead zone.

Cancel dreams
destroy temptation
world's vanished into the black hole
two big Macs to go
and a side order of what?
Check social media
for the answer to these and other
important questions.

We've been taught:
God created the world
and man
and woman
don't re-invent the wheel
little hope is better
than no hope at all
good boys and girls go to heaven —
hell must be bursting at the seams!

We are visual creatures now,
Teledroids
captivated by hypnotic signals of
tits
ass
violence
inane jokes
porcelain teeth
expensive wardrobes
make-up
lights
camera
action!
enriched
by occasional spots
of educational programming
magnanimously funded
by corporations
who hope very much
we don't mind them
polluting our air and water and lives.
Why should we?
we have cable!

Query:
Where are our minds?

Response:
Scattered like dried straw
stemming turbulent waters
bobbing for air —
not apples of knowledge
illusions of such.

Writing has devolved as trivial art
minimal as communication
and a technical
must study tiresome bore.

So why write?
es-special-ly cre-atively.

Every subject's been exploited:
love
war
poverty
religion
history
justice
injustice
insanity
sanity
thrills
dreams
killers
nightmares
sex and politics
politics and sex
he said
she said
they said
and we listen.
(For areas outside of creative writing
please consult your local library,
if you have one.)

As you are reading this,
understand?
Great writing often reflects
the diligent work of persons
mirroring people
in hopes of enlightening
while entertaining.

Sooooo!
There is nothing new left to write
and why should there be
when we have yet gotten
what little we know of ourselves right?
Write?

Legacy

No one springs
from womb
absent of tears
and needs.

No one loves
another
devoid of doubt
and greed.

No one strives
for self
vacuous of truth
and fear.

No one falls
to earth
oblivious of shame
and dreams.

Mortal Thoughts

Staring skyward at night-light
flickering stars yawn and wink
royal blue canvas eclipses daylight
moonlight on my bedspread plays.

If I could climb ethereal moonbeams
upward home to majestic gates,
there awaits a hallowed freedom
from my soul in current chains.

Repose my burdens on celestial altars
sacrifice my weathering flesh
pierce my heart, my will, my karma
with molten steel or feathered dirk.

Across a braying swaybacked mule
drape my organic putrid flesh;
immodest beast ascend Olympus
trust his footing and his trek.

On an Ass, I'll journey homeward
to the place from which we came
laid to rest at feet almighty
of a God with many names.

Fame

Fame is one of many
coveted components of life,
most immortal
of all mortal gifts.

It exists as elusive
transitory vapor
tantalizing every
and all who breathe.

Few among us capture
this treasured element —
those who do
attempt imprisonment
in their interpretation
of dream-tight jars.

Time drills holes
in plate brass lids
secured to these filigree jars,
allowing fame
silent passage home
to Obscurity.

Obscurity

Obscurity is a vaporous haunt,
antithesis abode of fame
where light is not a visible element
escaping before our laced membranes.

Fostered mortals apprehend this dwelling,
an elusive quintessential domain
where touch of hand and soul and body
are trapped within their own refrains.

Visionaries populate its turbid landscape,
anonymous specters existing unaware
of late night charades and evasive dark shapes,
metamorphic actors portraying time and despair.

Actors feeling blindly along stages,
hemorrhaging with strife, defiled by death,
beleaguered plays forever spiraling onward
within the inhalation of a shallow breath.

Mystery

Listen,
can you hear it?
A faint trill coo casting down
from diamond studded twilight,
riding brisk autumn winds.

Look,
can you see it?
An unruly light bursting
high above continents,
between clouds, amid forests,
beaming brilliant against all things.

Touch,
can you feel it?
A prickly cool sensation
stitching through your pores,
swimming about your flesh,
melting into your bones.

Smell,
has it scent?
A frisky fragrance parading
spicy, aromatic, a savory dish,
intriguing curiosity
en route to your palate.

Taste,
has it flavor?
Sweet, yet bitter,
meat, yet wine,
the grandest of feasts
enjoyed in a single bite.

Guess,
do you know it?
Is it of this place?

Freedom

What is it like to be free?
Relinquished from disparity
I mean totally, absolutely unchained.
Freedom, what might you be?

Are you the autumn leaf
floating tenderly on air,
or budding spring grass
stretching skyward to kiss the sun?

Are you a magnificent
rainbow bird
soaring from land to land,
universe in hand?

Is Freedom a cloud
Suspended in mortal space
drifting facilely,
from shadowed place to place?

Maybe you're the wind,
whisking arbitrarily about,
whirling temperate air,
existing everywhere.

Could you be the oceans?
Water's deep and wide,
moving without restraint,
in and out of tide.

Are you light?
Twinkling bright, dimly glowing,
intense, placid, warmly overflowing —
stumbling into night.

Are you night?
Silken, sweetly ominous,
like a huge black bear
laid to rest on dawn.

Perhaps you're flesh,
brawny, bold, defiant,
hurling wicked souls
hellward with a herculean toss.

Most simply you could be a tear
created in human eyes,
trickling crystal liquid
pulsing down elated cheeks.

Dare you swirl upon violent winds?
Swim deep beneath angry seas?
Wherever do you wonder?
Whatever might you be?

I implore you grasp my soul,
whisper deep in solemn ears.
Guide me to your holy land,
for man's sake, let freedom live!

Eyes shut tight to all persuasions
ears clamped deaf to every wile
greatest secret of all secrets
from me none will secure.

Let me traipse your sacred ground,
breathe air that is of you,
sip water from your well,
taste your ripened, precious fruit.

All I need is confirmation
not fictitious tales of youth.

If indeed you are true being,
life would not seem so cruel.
For each day, my soul could savor
blessed memories shared with you.

Justice

Arise peaceful giant to claim what is rightfully yours.

Far too long your words have been whispers
engulfed in the callous winds
of deprivation and persecution.

Let your magnificent voice resound
above mountains ranges
to be carried by clouds of humanity

to every crevice of the world.

Speak out until your laws are lasers
piercing through darkened minds
of those deaf with iniquities.

Only after the ignorant are enlightened
shall it be safe for you to rest.

Suspended For A Moment

Calmness serenely dozes
firmly entrenched
within the tepid
docile womb of silence.

Tranquil voices hum
in heavenly harmony
overflowing
contemplations' chalice.

Visions swirl passionately
above Realities' constrictors
funneling harmlessly
far out of mind.

Time views inertly
the fragile being
behind pellucid walls
it cannot penetrate.

Confusion

I don't know.
What?
The answer.
What's the question?
Don't know.
What?
Anything — everything.
Who does?
God, I guess.
Who knows God?
Don't know.
So what's the point?
Exactly.

Our Trek

Our world
dreary and bright
dreadful with plight
of mortal men.

Our land
barren and rich
cursed by the hand
father nature's plan.

Our homes
anguish and hope
ragged love curtains
shield windows of despair.

Our dreams
dwindle and sparkle
deep within souls
of children while sleeping.

Our lives
overflowing and empty
believing in few
while trusting in none.

Our deaths
young and old
wishing to hold
onto life ever fleeting.

Our spirits
shackled and free
refusing the steed
saddled by destiny.

Our trek
relenting and spent
engulfed in the flames
to begin once again.

Escape

Society demands much
of so small a person
in momentary possession
of tiny human hands
pinned beneath huge needs
prodding a sane psyche
to tug harder on the life-chord
for permanent escape.

Lake

He kneels before a lake.
Mirrored
in its taciturn surface
himself
gazing at
the great aphonic vault
and beyond.

Virgins

Blessed virgins are we all
we know so little of life.

Life

None is capable of saddling life.
Almost everyone tries
at some point in their reality,
factual experiences
pooling as distorted biographies.

Aspirations

With each passing day
hope meanders away
dreams yet realized
wave in the distance,
swaying willows
still in sight
vestal brides to be.

Contentment

I have banished the idea of happiness,
I'll settle for contentment.

Integrity

We speak of honesty and truth
as virtues rooted in granite,
not transitory substances,
pliable as gelatin,
elusive as colors to the blind.

Change

Consciousness nudges,
lethargy,
who rises . . .
stimulated nipples
upon the swarthy breasts
of conviction.

Blood

Young blood looking to alter the world,
old blood seeking a place to rest.

Moving

Their lives, their loves, their memories
were neatly documented
by photographs and journals
left behind when they relocated.

Summer

Lavish
radiant
chimeric prose
sultry greetings
lazy hopes
fantasies flutter
from crimson skies
enchantment nocturnal
lifts veils from her eyes
patrolling dream-mist
she walks forth to savor
days long in ceasing
nights clothed in sable.

Morning Sun

The very first day
he opened his eyes
to see the morning sun;
to his very first step,
his very first word,
the learning had just begun.
He went off to school
to learn a bit more
from books or in the streets.
Slowly he grew
to achieve the things
of the man he was meant to be.
The knowledge came
both quick and slow;
sooner or later, he got it.
Then came the time
he was out on his own
in a world he hoped to inspire.
Working five days a week,
forty hours in all,
responsibility stoked the fire.
And just as his folks
married, had children,
and created a comfortable empire.
Now the years rifled by
at a blistering rate,
his children followed their yearnings;
with a turn of his head,
they were out on their own,
while he made most of his earnings.
Reflecting on this
in a hospital bed,
there welled a tear in his eye.
He longed for the time,
far-gone days of youth,
when his only limit was sky.

Turning to glance
out the window, he spied
the brilliant morning sun.
Faintly he smiled,
eased shut his eyes,
and offered his soul to God ...

to be reborn.

Relationships

At times, I peer
so far into the future
I cannot see today.
Is the sun shining?

Tomorrow's shadow pounds
his mirrored tomb
screeching at deaf yesterday
who is pondering
irreversible mistakes.

Time,
in flaming-eyed mockery,
dictates:
Creation! Build a new world!
Destruction! Make way the path!
Evolution! Assure constant change!

Forge high these common trusses
that all may stride across
sparkling waters leaping
engulfing blustering clouds
in ceaseless
futile flight.

Is there immortality?

Being

I am:
a lover
a friend
passion deep within,
circle and line,
mirror blind
vision bright
dreamer, realist
genius and fool,
mountains of pleasure
chasms of pain
captive, freedom
water and flame
universe, atom
pride and shame,
tear, smile
goodness and hate
question, answer
birth and fate.
You may ask
what is my name.
It is plain and simple.
I am Man.

Autumn

Red and plum
gold and green
paint sincere
miraculous scenes
dismembered leaves
defenseless spirals
scurry wayward
with vagabond soil
toward burial grounds
for hibernating souls.

Night Bird

On my windowsill
rests a night bird
warbling to
a pocked-faced moon
inquiring in
its trilling tune,
"Must Ra mask
himself with you
from a world bereft
and drenched in sin?"

Calm

Peace and quiet,
the sort that invades
each unoccupied strain
of gray matter,
flows, resonates, disperses
to be greedily sponged by
an insatiable psyche.

If you listen intuitively,
you can hear the earth yawn,
stretch and breath,
witness where the dove
rides the lion,
feel icicle fingers
massaging mortal omens.

Hope

Where there is hope
there is life,
once all embers of hope
are extinguished,
what remains are the dark
cold caldrons of remorseless loss

when the glowing embers
of hope turn cold,
their bitter dry ash
weeping into desolate ground,
becoming fossils of repentant death
lacking nourishment for the living.

Talkin' Crazy

Endocrine within our galaxy
a world rumored to exist
where dreams retain more status
than sleep-conjured images
hovering in a dewy mist.

Within our far stretched universe
of planets, stars and sun
abides a settlement where all are one
quite equal to the grudging task
of judging all with fairness and tact,

a far-flung roadstead
where measure of worth
is not counterbalanced
against material wealth
but fullness of heart
and bounty of soul.

If by some marvel —
Miracle, no doubt —
this fabled, foretold world resides
outside the interminable region
of our fragile planet's nest

perhaps it will migrate
near one day
mercifully orbiting
our desperate sphere
raining concordant radiance

to bathe in
to drink up
to succor the strife
which nullifies our understanding
and fouls compassion's breath.

As placid as celestial light
this globe shall arrive
to alter our plight
before that pathetic day
when mankind will cease.

Far be it from me
to believe such rantings
is foolish indeed,
mankind could never elevate
above their Neanderthal creed —

or so it seems —
since exorbitant energy is spent
causing fellow humans duress.
Oh, don't mind me.
I'm just *talkin' crazy.*

Sorrow Wish

I wish I could discover words
to lift your sorrow from its grave
or gift a song to soothe your heart
rebuking anguish for being born.

What offer I is a shoulder strong
to liberate your engorged burdens,
fond arms to hug you close and safe,
protection from the lashing throng;

gentle hands to banish wicked tears
from tender skin into oblivion,
bottomless wells of kind patient ears
to spill your buckets of suffering;

a heart to commiserate with your own
pumping helium words as wings to soar,
corpuscles of sanguinity and bliss and resurrection
construct a platform of solid acceptance;

tomorrow will rise and you will become
stalwart, perseverant, amnestic and remissive,
the next day will follow, as will the next,
delivered from rapids and chaotic cliffs.

Your drowning spirit preserved from despair
buoyed aloft on shoals of bright memories,
a tranquil craft forged true and strong
to knife its way through raging misery.

Will God Return?

When our world evolves
from arid nomad lands
to glacier mountain ranges,
its dour face
toward a blinding sun,
its shadowy back
watched by the moon.

Will God return?

Will love be his rule?

Womb of Time

Tomorrow's mystic illusions
cemented by foregone days,
are faint heartbeat tremors
in bedrock paths of claim.

Blind soldiers march defiant
along vast plains of Time;
bootless pallbearers gathered
burying each before in line.

Eclipse

From dust of dawn
came life in man
in twilight stars
where his soul began
heaven sent
to bloodied lands
hopefully
a redemptive plan.

Limitations

Borders, barricades, boundaries,
                literal metaphors
Auto Body Paint Shop
                delineate creative virtuosity
Artificial Limb Company
                in iambic expressions
Freedom in Black History
                as lily pads in a snow storm
displayed in the White Gallery
                music, literature, poetry and art
she waded through the crowd
                musing precipitous meaning
pursing her lips
                attempting to comprehend it all.

Notes

Rhyming Poetry references "The Vision of Judgment" by George Gordon Byron (Lord Byron).

Acknowledgements

Thanks to the editors and staff of the following publications, living and deceased, where some of these offerings first found a home:

Ital Effect, Issue 2, August 1998 (Imagination)

Bare Bones & Bylines, Golden Apple Press (Rhyming Poetry)

More Big Thoughts, Golden Apple Press (Flattery, Fatigue, Accomplishments)

Opening Windows, Golden Apple Press (Morning Sun, Dreams)

Mentor Magazine, Fall Issue 1996 (Being)

Poetry Motel Wallpaper, Suburban Wilderness, (Confusion)

To Climb A Purple Mountain, Golden Apple Press (Our Trek, Aspirations, Legacy)

The Robin's Nest, Pometaphysics Publishing (Unwelcome Visitor)

Little Verse-Big Thoughts, Golden Apple Press (Body Count, Virgins)

The Color of Gold, Golden Apple Press (Winter, Spring, Summer, Autumn)

On The Threshold of a Dream, The National Library of Poetry (Grandma)

Loose Gravel, Vol. 1, No. 1, Summer 1988, (Freedom)

Michael R Lane was born and raised in Pittsburgh, Pennsylvania. Michael studied English Literature and Creative Writing at Point Park University, Sonoma State University, and Portland State University in an effort to hone his craft. He has written poetry for more than three decades, and has had poetry published in numerous journals.

www.ingramcontent.com/pod-product-compliance
Lightning Source LLC
Chambersburg PA
CBHW020318130626
46549CB00003B/924